Topsy-Turvy

Arabia Pictured for Children

Amy E. Zwemer

Samuel Marinus Zwemer

Alpha Editions

This edition published in 2024

ISBN : 9789357956819

Design and Setting By
Alpha Editions
www.alphaedis.com
Email - info@alphaedis.com

Contents

PREFACE

This is a book of pictures and stories for big children and small grown-up folks; for all who love Sinbad the sailor and his strange country. It is a topsy-turvy book; there is no order about the chapters; and you can begin to read it anywhere. It is intended to give a bird's-eye view to those who cannot take birds' wings. The stories are not as good as those of the Arabian Nights but the morals are better—and so are the pictures. Moreover the stories are true. You must not skip any of the chapters or the pictures but you may the preface, if you like.

{S.M.Z.
{A.E.Z.

Bahrein, Arabia.

I
WHY IS ARABIA TOPSY-TURVY LAND?

On this big round earth there are all sorts of countries and peoples. Men walk on it on every side just like flies crawling over a watermelon and they do not fall off either. On the next page you can see how they travel all around the world; some in steamships, some in carriages or on horses, some in jinrickshaws and some in the railway coaches. In Topsy-turvy Land they have no railroads and not even waggon-roads or waggons. A horse or a camel or a donkey is used for passengers and the camel caravan is a freight train.

Or if you wish, the camel is a topsy-turvy ship which sails in the sand instead of in the water. It is called the ship of the desert. The masts point down instead of up; there are four masts instead of three; and although there are ropes the desert-ship has no sails and no rudder—unless the rudder be the tail. When the ship lies at anchor to be loaded it feeds on grass and the four masts are all snugly tucked away under the hull. In Arabia you generally see these ships of the desert in a long line like a naval procession, each battleship towing its mate by a piece of rope fastened from halter to tail! But not only is the mode of travel strange in Topsy-turvy Land, even the time of the day is all upside down. When the boys and girls of America are going to bed the boys and girls of Arabia are thinking of getting up. As early as four o'clock by western time the muezzin calls out loud from the top of the minaret (for Moslem churches have no steeples and no bells) to come and pray. Arabs count the hours from sunrise. It is noon at six o'clock and they breakfast at one; at three o'clock in the evening all good boys and girls are asleep.

MODES OF TRAVEL.

In Topsy-turvy Land all the habits and customs are exactly opposite to those in America or England. For instance when a boy enters a room he takes off his shoes but leaves his hat on his head. I do not know whether we should call it a *hat*, however. His hat has no rim and is not made of felt or straw, but is just a folded handkerchief of a large size and bright colour with a piece of cord to hold it wound round his head—a sort of a hat in two pieces. The girls go without shoes but carefully cover their pretty (or ugly) faces with a black veil.

At home you eat with a spoon or use a knife and fork. Here the Arabs eat with their fingers; nor do they use any plates or butter dishes, but a large piece of flat bread serves as a plate until it is all eaten. So you see in Arabia the children not only eat their rice and meat but their plates also. You read a book from left to right but in Arabia everybody begins at the right-hand cover and reads backward. Even the lines read backward and in Arabic writing there are no commas or capitals and the vowels are written not next to the consonants but stuck up above them. *Potato* in Arabic would be written with English letters this way:

O	A	O
T	T	P

Can you read it?

In your country a carpenter stands at his bench to work, but here they sit on the ground. With you he uses a vise to hold the board or stick he is planing; here he uses his bare toes. With you he *pushes* the saw or, especially, the plane away from him to cut or to smooth a piece of wood, but in Topsy-turvy Land he *pulls* his tools towards him. Buttons are on the button-hole side and the holes are where you put the buttons. Door keys and door hinges are made of wood, not of iron as in the Occident. The women wear toe-rings and nose-rings as well as earrings and bracelets. Everything seems different from what it is in a Christian country.

One strange sight is to meet people out riding. Do you know that the men ride donkeys side-saddle, but the women ride as men do in your country? When a missionary lady first came to Bahrein in Eastern Arabia and the boys saw her riding a donkey they called out: *"Come and see, come and see! The lady has no feet!"* Because they saw only one side of her. Then another one called out and said: *"Yes she has, and they are both on this side!"*

EUROPEAN VISITORS ON DONKEYS.

Another odd custom is that Arabs always turn the fingers of the hand down as we turn them up in beckoning or calling anybody. Many other gestures seem topsy-turvy as well.

In your country boys learn the lesson of politeness—ladies first; but it is not so over here. It is *men first* in all grades of society; and not only men first but men last, in the middle, and all the time. Women and girls have a very small place given them in Topsy-turvy Land. The Arabs say that of all animal kinds the female is the most valuable except in the case of mankind! When a girl baby is born the parents are thought very unfortunate. How hard the Bedouin girls have to work! They are treated just like beasts of burden as if they had no souls. They go barefoot carrying heavy loads of wood or skins of water, grind the meal and make fresh bread every morning or spin the camel's hair or goat's hair into one coarse garment. They are very ignorant and superstitious, the chief remedies for sickness being to brand the body with a hot iron or wear charms—a verse from the Koran sewn up in leather or a string of blue beads, which are supposed to drive away evil influences.

How very thankful girls should be that in all Christian lands they have a higher place and a better lot than the poor girls and women of Arabia! For the greatest contrast is the religion of the inhabitants of Topsy-turvy Land. That is all upside down too. The Lord Jesus teaches us to pray in secret not to be seen of men; we are to go quietly alone and tell God everything. But Mohammed, the prophet of Arabia, taught his followers to pray openly on any street corner, or on the deck of a ship, in public, just like the Pharisees whom Jesus condemns. And when these people fast, as they are supposed to for a whole month, they do not really go without food, but each day at *sunset* they begin to eat in larger quantity than usual!—because they think by such fasting to gain favour with God and do not know that to fast from sin and evil habits is the fast God wants. Another thing very sad in this land of Topsy-turvy is that there are no Sunday-schools—they do not observe our Sabbath—and the boys and girls do not have bright Sunday-school lesson leaves or a picture-roll. They spend Sunday and every other day in learning all the evil they see in those that are grown up. Poor children! They have never heard the sweet words of Jesus, "Suffer little children to come unto me and forbid them not: for of such is the kingdom of God." We tell you all this about them that you may pray for them that God may soon send more missionaries to preach to them these precious words. We want you all by prayer and offerings to help put a silver lining in the dark clouds of their lives.

The other chapters in this little book will tell you more about the land and its people and as you read them do not forget to pray for them.

If you are faithful and true, always shining for Jesus, your bright light will reach as far as dark Arabia, and will help to turn that land of Topsy-turvy right side up. When joy and gladness will take the place of sorrow and sadness, and ignorance give way to the knowledge of the Truth. In one place in the Bible it tells how to make these topsy-turvy lands right side up again. Do you know where that is? Acts 17:6-7. "*These that have turned the world upside down are come hither also ... saying that there is another King, even* JESUS."

II
A LESSON IN GEOGRAPHY

In the atlas Arabia looks like a big mail-pouch hung up by the side of some railway station, pretty empty of everything. But this queer mail-pouch country is not as empty as people imagine. It is a country larger than all of the United States east of the Mississippi. It is longer than the longest mail-pouch and much wider. From north to south you can ride a camel one thousand miles and from east to west more than six hundred. But the geography of the country is topsy-turvy altogether and that is why it has been so long a neglected peninsula. People kept on wondering at the queer exterior of the mail-pouch and never opened the lock to its secrets by looking into the interior.

First of all, Arabia is perhaps the only land that has three of its boundaries fixed and the other always shifting. Such is the case with the northern boundary of Arabia. It is different on every map and changes every year because the inhabitants go about as nomads; that is, they "have no continuing city."

Arabia has no rivers except underground. It has no railroad and very few roads at all. Some parts of the country are very green and fertile and in other parts there is not enough grass the year around to give one square meal to a single grasshopper. Arabia has four thousand miles of coast and yet only six harbours where steamers call. There are better maps of the North Pole and of Mars and of the moon than of southeastern Arabia. The reason is that men have spent millions of dollars to find the North Pole and telescopes are all the time looking at the moon; but no one has ever spent time or money to explore this part of Arabia. The Greek geographers had a better knowledge of Arabia than we have to-day.

MAP OF ARABIA.

There are no lakes in Arabia, but there is a large sea of sand called *Al Ahkaf,* in which the traveller Von Wrede threw a lead and line and found no bottom! No one has been there since to see whether his story was true. At Bahrein, in eastern Arabia, there are salt-water wells on shore and fresh-water springs in the midst of the salt sea from which water is brought to shore. Arabia has no postage-stamps and no political capital and no telegraph system. Different coins from different parts of the world are used in different provinces. It is a land of contradictions and even the waters that bound it are misnamed. The Red Sea is blue; the Persian Gulf has no Persian ships and should be called an English lake; and the *Straits* of Hormuz are crooked. This topsy-turvy land has no political divisions. Some say it has five and some seven provinces; no one knows what is its population as no census was ever taken. In nearly all countries the mountain ranges run north and south, but in Arabia they run nearly east and west. There are desert sands six hundred feet deep and mountain peaks nine thousand feet high. On the coasts it is fearfully hot and the climate is often deadly. On the highlands it is often bitterly cold; and yet the people are all of the same race and speech and custom and language and religion.

READY FOR A CAMEL RIDE.

There are no pumps in Arabia, but plenty of wells. There are no woods in Arabia, but plenty of trees. The camel is a topsy-turvy ship and the ostrich a topsy-turvy bird. The Arabs call the former the ship of the desert; and the latter they say is half camel and half bird. In some parts of Arabia horses and cows are fed on boiled fish because that is cheaper than grass! In other parts of the country donkeys are fed on dates. Arabia has more sultans and princes than any other country of the same size and yet it is a land without a settled government. The people never meet one another without saying "Peace to you"; yet there has never been any peace over the whole land since Christ's birth or even since the days of Ishmael.

Every one carries a weapon and yet there are very few wild animals. It is more dangerous to meet a Bedouin than a lion when you are a stranger on the road. The Arabs are a nation of robbers. Now you will wonder how we can also say that Orientals are the most hospitable of any people in the world for the Arabs are Orientals. And yet it is strictly true that these robbers are more hospitable, in a way, than you people of Western countries. They have a proverb which says that "Every stranger is an invited guest"; and another which says, "The guest while in the house is its lord." If an Arab gets after you to rob or kill you, it is only necessary to take refuge in his tent for safety. He is bound then, by the rules of Oriental hospitality, to treat you as his guest. But you must not stay there too long and you must be careful how you get away! You will find instances of this respect for the duty of hospitality all through the Bible story. It was in the earliest Bible times, as later and as now, a grievous sin to be inhospitable. The cradle of the Mohammedan religion is Arabia, and yet in no country are they more ignorant of their religion. How sad to think that when they do worship God they do it in such an ignorant and idolatrous way! In our next chapter we shall see more about this.

Arabia has no national flag, no national hymn and no national feeling. Every one lives for himself and no one cares for his neighbour. This does not sound strange of robbers but it does of people who are so hospitable. This queer country we are about to visit together and talk over with each other.

You will not grow weary by the way, we hope. If the desert tracks are long and tiresome through the following chapters, just refresh yourself in the oasis of a picture.

III
THE SQUARE-HOUSE WITH THE BLACK OVERCOAT

You think I am making fun but it is really true that in western Arabia there is a house that always wears an overcoat. This is a large, square stone house without windows and with only one door to let in the light and the air; it is empty inside, although crowds gather around it as you see in the picture. Yet this house always has on an overcoat of black silk, very heavy and richly embroidered. Every year the old coat is taken off and a new one put on. A few days ago a Moslem pilgrim showed me a piece of the cloth of last year's overcoat and he was very proud of it. It was indeed a fine piece of heavy silk and the names of God and Mohammed were prettily woven into the cloth. This man had just come from visiting the square-house and I will tell you what he saw.

The place he visited with hundreds and thousands of other pilgrims is called Mecca and the square-house is the *Beit Allah* or house of God to all Mohammedans. It is also called the *Kaaba*, which is the Arabic word for a cube.

The Moslems believe all sorts of foolish things about the Kaaba. They say Adam built it as soon as he fell down on the earth out of Paradise, and that Abraham repaired it after it had been ruined by the flood in the days of Noah. They even show a large white stone on which Abraham and Ishmael stood when they plastered the walls; the stone still bears the impress of Abraham's feet, they say. Did you ever hear such a topsy-turvy story?

The building is about twenty-four cubits long and wide and nearly twenty cubits high. It has no ornaments or beauty except one rain-spout to carry the water off the flat roof; you can see it on the right side of the Kaaba on the picture. This spout is said to be of pure gold. In one corner of the building is a large black stone which is also an object of worship. The Mohammedans say it came down from heaven with Adam and was once pure white. By the many kisses of sinful worshippers it has turned black. Not only is it black but broken. For about three hundred years after Mohammed's death the stone remained imbedded in the walls of the Kaaba, but then some wild Arabs from the Persian Gulf came, sacked Mecca and stole the black stone. It was carried to Katif, a place near Bahrein, right across Arabia, and they kept it a long time until the people of Mecca paid a large sum of money and carried it back. On the long journey it must have fallen from the camel because, at present, it is cracked and the broken pieces are held together by a silver band. There once were a great many of these stone idols in the Kaaba, but

Mohammed destroyed them all except this one when he became master of Mecca.

THE SQUARE HOUSE WITH THE BLACK OVERCOAT.

At present the stone house is empty of idols and yet all the Moslems turn in the direction of this old heathen temple to pray. The cloth that covers it comes every year as a present from the Khedive of Egypt, who is a Mohammedan. It is very costly and is sent on a special camel, beautifully decked with trappings of gilt, and a large throng of pilgrims go along to escort the overcoat.

When the wind stirs the heavy folds of cloth, the pious boys and girls of Mecca say it is the angels that watch around the Kaaba, whose wings lift the covering. It must be a wonderful sight to see thousands of Moslem pilgrims stand around this place and kneel and pray.

Besides running around the Kaaba, kissing the black stone and drinking water from a holy well called *zemzem*, they have one day on which they sacrifice sheep or other animals. One curious custom on this day of sacrifice I must tell you of. It is called "stoning the great devil." Early in the morning thousands of pilgrims go to a place in the valley of Mina where there are three white pillars made of masonry; the first and largest is called the Great Devil. The pilgrims cast stones at this pillar. Each one must stand at the distance of not less than fifteen feet and say, as he throws seven pebbles: "In the name of God the Almighty I do this, and in hatred of the devil and his shame." The Moslems fail to realise that Satan is in the hearts of men and not behind a pillar, nor that he can be driven away with prayer better than by pebbles.

For thirteen hundred years Moslems have come every year to Mecca, and gone away, with no one ever to tell them of the Son of God, the Saviour of the World. Thirteen hundred years! Don't you think it is time to go and tell them? And will you not pray that even this place may open its doors to Jesus Christ, and crown Him Lord of all?

IV
SABBACH-KUM BIL KHEIR!

That is to say, "Good-morning!" And the Arabs in the picture do not add, "have you used Pears' Soap?" but, "have you had your cup of Mocha coffee?" Soap is a luxury in most parts of Arabia and the vast majority of its inhabitants never use it; millions would not know it if they saw it. Perhaps the old Sheikh, however, used a bit of soap to wash his hands and feet early before sunrise when he went to the mosque to pray. Now he has returned and sits in the coffee-shop ready to take a sip of coffee and "drink tobacco" from the long pipe. The Arabs always speak of *drinking* tobacco when they mean to smoke; I suppose one reason is because they use the peculiar water-pipes with the long stems in which the smoke passes through the water and bubbles out to the mouth. Have you time to stop and study the picture with me?

What a pretty window in the corner! The Arabs call a window *shibaak*, which means network, because their windows are very much like a fish-net. Glass is seldom used in Arabia except by Europeans and Arabs who have become civilised; and so the carpenter or joiner fits little round bars, one into the other, like marbles or beads on a string and the result is often very beautiful. Light and air come in (not to speak of clouds of dust) while no one can look through from the outside; and you know how afraid Arab girls and women are to show their faces to strangers.

Under the arch is the open fireplace where the big coffee-pots and water-kettles simmer all day on a charcoal fire. The old man looks quite cheerful seated on his uncomfortable stool made of date-sticks. You will read later about our old friend the date-palm and how the tree is used for nearly every purpose. I wish I could show you how they take the thin branches and punch holes in them and then deftly, before you can count ninety, build together a chair or a bedstead. I have often slept soundly and safely on bedsteads made of these thin leaf-sticks no bigger around than a child's finger. The sticks are full of "spring" so one does not need a wire mattress, nor have I ever known one of them, if made honestly, to become a *folding bed* under a restless sleeper as they say happens sometimes in New York hotels!

Although the old man in our picture is waited on by the younger Arab (who is perhaps the keeper of the café), yet I know he is not rich. Do you notice his toil-worn hands and the patch on the shoulder of his long overcoat? I fancy too his pretty vest, so carefully buttoned by more than a dozen cloth buttons, is a little torn on one side; nor has he a fine girdle like the rich shopkeepers.

SABBACH-KUM BIL KHEIR!

Extremes meet in the picture and three countries widely apart on the map are brought close together. Of course, you know the coffee is the real Yemen article, which coming first from Mocha on the Red Sea, is still called by that Arabian name. The curious pipe with its round bottom, carved head-piece and long stem, is used everywhere in Arabia and is generally called *"nargeelie,"* which is the Indian name for cocoanut. The bowl of the pipe is in fact an empty cocoanut shell; the stem once grew in the jungle and perhaps tigers brushed past it; now it is pierced to draw smoke.

The curious pipe is from India, the tobacco first came from America but the coffee is Arabian. Let us listen to the story of the cup of coffee: In a book published in 1566 by an Arab scholar on the virtues of coffee it is stated that a knowledge of coffee was first brought to Arabia from Abyssinia about the year 1400 by a pious man whose tomb is still venerated in Yemen. The knowledge of coffee spread from Yemen in south Arabia over the whole world. In 1690 Van Hoorne, a general of the Dutch East India company, received a few coffee seeds from the Arabs at Mocha and planted them in Batavia on the island of Java. In this way Mocha coffee has become the mother of Java and of all other kinds of coffee sold at your grocers'. Nothing can be more beautiful than the green hills and fertile gardens in the Arabian coffee country. The coffee berry grows on an evergreen tree of about eighteen feet high; its leaves are a beautiful dark, shining green and the blossom of the tree is pure white with a most delicate and fragrant odour. Each tree bears an enormous number of coffee-berries; a single tree is said to have yielded sixteen pounds! Arabia not only produces the finest coffee in the world, but I think the Arabs know how to prepare a good cup of coffee better than other peoples. The raw bean is roasted just before it is used and so keeps all its strength; it is *pounded* fine, much finer than you can grind it, in a mortar, with an iron pestle; lastly two smelling herbs, *heyl* and saffron are added when it is boiled just enough to give a flavour. Some fibres of palm bark are stuck into the spout of the coffee-pot to act as a strainer and then the clear brown liquid is poured into a tiny cup and handed to you in the coffee-shop. No wonder the Arab dervishes smack their lips over this, their only luxury.

But how did the tobacco get into our picture? You can hunt up the story for yourselves in your school histories. Had not Sir Walter Raleigh in 1586 introduced the weed to the court of Queen Elizabeth from Virginia, our picture and social life in Arabia would be very different. The custom of puffing tobacco has spread like a prairie fire and it is now so common in the East that very few realise it was not always found there. There they are all together, an Indian pipe, Arabian coffee and American tobacco! How much faster and further tobacco has travelled than the Bible; how many people had begun to drink Mocha before Arabia had a missionary!

But, of course, nothing can travel for nothing; and somebody must pay the travelling expenses. America pays many millions more for tobacco in a year than it pays for missionaries. It is not surprising, therefore, that all Arabians smoke and only a very few have ever heard of the Son of God, the Saviour of the world. As Jesus Himself said, "the children of this world are wiser in their generation than the children of light." When people learn to love missions as much and as often as they do a good cigar and a cup of coffee there will be no need of mite boxes. God hasten the day.

V
AT THE CORNER GROCERY

It is not a very long distance from the Arab coffee-shop where we left our friend smoking, to the grocer. The streets are very narrow and unless we are very careful that camel will crowd us to the wall or those water-skins on the white donkey wet our clothes—see how they drip! Well, one turn more and here we are. The grocer in the picture on the next page is leaning on his elbow waiting for a customer. And if he keeps his groceries as free from flies and ants as he does his spotless white turban we will buy our day's supplies here. The shops in Arabia are not very large and they have no place for customers except outside. Sometimes there is a sort of raised seat or bench on which the purchaser sits when he bargains for something; but generally you have to stand up outside while the crowds push and the traffic goes on. One curious custom is that all the shops of one kind cluster close together in one street or section of the town. You will see for example in one street a long row of shops where they sell drugs and perfumery; in another place there are only hardware merchants; again a whole street of nothing but grocers. I think the reason is that Arabs love to bargain and to beat down prices and so it is easier to have all the merchants of one kind close together. At any rate this arrangement makes it quite convenient for the purchaser. Indeed it is becoming somewhat customary to group the shops in this way in some of your Western cities. Occidental civilisation can learn some things from the Orient!

ARAB GROCER.

Our shopkeeper has a mixed lot of groceries in his shop; many things which you would find at your grocers' he has never heard of. Everything is topsy-turvy. Just fancy how strange to hang up the sugar in a row of cones on strings like sausages! Do you see them on the ceiling of the shop in our picture? That is the way white sugar comes wrapped from France and is sold in Arabia. A sugar *barrel* would soon be full of ants in this country; but when it hangs up on a string the ants have a hard time getting it away. Maybe there is a suggestion here for your homes if you are troubled with ants.

In those big Arab baskets the grocer keeps his carrots and other vegetables; carrots are white in Arabia and there are curious vegetables of which you have never heard.

Do you see the bottles and tin boxes on his shelves? Those are for spices; pepper, cinnamon, nutmegs, curry-powder and such things of which Arab housewives are very fond.

The big bowl on the left probably has olives in it or other kind of pickled vegetables. On the right you can see the big pair of old fashioned scales on which he weighs his wares. I hope he is an honest man, although I do not think he looks very honest, do you? The scale hangs true I have no doubt; but it is in the weights that deception lurks. In Arabia we can every day see illustrations of the words of Solomon in the book of Proverbs about "divers weights" and "false balances." The most of the shopkeepers do not have proper weights of iron or brass, but use ordinary cobblestones and pebbles. Only a few days ago I bought some walnuts and the grocer weighed them so many stones' weight! Do you know what a "stone" weight is. Maybe you had better look it up in your dictionary. That covered kettle near the scale-pans on top of the little box contains *semn*, which is the Arabic name for sheep's fat. You would hardly believe me if I told you what a lot of this greasy yellow stuff the boys and girls eat on their rice, and how much is used in an Arab kitchen. It is sold by weight, just as well as all other things, even *milk* in Arabia. If we wait long enough you will see Fatimah and Mirjam and the other girls come with empty bowls to buy so many pennies' worth of grease.

Do you notice that the shop has queer little doors on the lower part of the front opening? The other part of the shop is closed by a flap-door that does not show on the picture. This is hinged from the top and is used when the shop is open as a sort of blind to keep off the sun or the rain.

When the shopkeeper leaves his shop for a half hour or so he hangs a sort of fish-net over the opening of his shop and never needs to lock it. This is a curious custom, and I have often wondered how the shops were safe from stealing boys or robbers in such cases. It is one more instance of how different the East is from the West.

The shopkeepers generally close their shops at sunset, and only in a very few places are there people who buy and sell or go about to do shopping by lamplight. Our grocer on the corner has provided for emergencies, and the large Arabian lantern ought to light up all his little shop.

Across the street is the place where they sell crockery. The salesman is out, but his boy, as you see, has taken the opportunity to eat some apples. I wonder whether he got them at the grocer's?

ARAB BOY IN A CROCKERY SHOP.

His father sells water-jugs and jars made of porous earth. Oh what a blessing those jars are to all the people of this hot and dry country. We have no ice in Arabia and so no refrigerators; the wells are never very deep and the water comes a long distance. So if it were not for the crockery man and his water-jugs we could never drink *cold* water. But just pour the water in one of these earthen pots and hang it in the wind and then in a few minutes the water gets cold. We missionaries always have such water-jars hanging or standing in our windows to catch the breeze. Perhaps this kind of water-cooler is very old, and Solomon himself looked at one when he wrote the words: "As cold waters to a thirsty soul so is good news from a far country."

VI
BLIND FATIMAH

It was on a Sunday afternoon that I first met Blind Fatimah and greeted her with *Salaam aleikum* and she answered *aleikum es salaam!* "Peace be to you and on you be peace." I asked if she could read. She said she could "read by heart," but could not see anything. She at that time could repeat twenty-six chapters of the Koran, the sacred book of the Mohammedans. Now I think she can repeat it nearly all; it contains one hundred and fourteen chapters. Some are very short and others are very long; some parts of the book are very good, but most of it is a jumble of events and of things that never happened—all mixed up topsy-turvy.

A slave woman was Fatimah's teacher and now she is helper in the school of this teacher. She is the prompter, and always begins each sentence of the recitation, and the other children follow on. If any mistakes are made, she will instantly correct them.

She is a peculiar looking girl and she is not pretty. Her clothes consist of cast off garments given her by others. Her head is generally covered and wrapped up in a black muslin veil; then she has an *abba* or Arabian cloak of very green-black cashmere; then under that a many coloured garment called a *thobe*; it is square in pattern with armholes and sleeves nearly a yard wide. The ends of these wide sleeves are deftly taken and thrown over the head to form a sort of tight-fitting cap. Underneath this garment is a kind of dressing gown with tight-fitting sleeves. Such is Fatimah's wardrobe. She wears no shoes, not even sandals. Would you like to walk in the hot sand with no covering for your feet?

Sometimes I visit the school where Fatimah teaches the smaller girls A, B, C. It is a topsy-turvy school indeed. The object seems to be to make as much noise as possible; the pupils sit on the floor with a small stand or trestle (like a saw-buck!) in front of each one to hold their Korans out of which they read. The first pupil begins a sentence at the top of his, or her, voice and then in a sort of refrain it is taken up by all the others. The teacher sits outside the school very often sewing or preparing a meal or entertaining visitors; for the schoolhouse is an ordinary mat hut dwelling. If however a pupil makes a mistake in reading she hears instantly and corrects it.

When the hours of prayer come around (the Moslems you know pray five times a day) lessons are dropped. One day I called at the school at the time of afternoon prayer. All the children had run down to the sea, to wash their faces and hands and feet, so as to be quite pure outwardly, when repeating Mohammed's prayers.

In the accompanying picture of a Moslem boy praying you will see what those forms are and how much *form* there is to go through. Blind Fatimah stood with her hands clasped, looking upward with those sightless eyes, her lips moving. Then she fell on her knees, with the little, thin hands spread out; then she bowed down until her forehead touched the earth, continuing in that position for a little time; then she got up, and with another upward look and motion of the lips, the devotions were ended.

HOW A MOSLEM BOY PRAYS.

I prayed there, too, that her eyes might be opened to see Jesus as her own Saviour, and that she might know Him as the *Son of God*, and not merely as one of the many prophets mentioned in the Koran. It seemed such a sad sight to see this blind child, doubly blind because her religion is false, and she is resting on a false hope.

She always listens when I tell her, or read to her about God, and Jesus Christ the Saviour. And if you would help together by your daily prayers, perhaps soon God will give the answer. Would it not be blessed for you and me if some day blind Fatimah should have opened eyes; not to see the date groves, and the sea, and the beautiful sunsets of Bahrein, but far more—to see Jesus' face and to follow Him by leading others to Him?

"For thousands and thousands who wander and fall,
Never heard of that heavenly home;
I should like them to know there is room for them all,
And that Jesus has bid them to come.
I long for the joy of that glorious time,
The sweetest and brightest and best,
When the dear little children of every clime
Shall crowd to His arms and be blest."

VII
DATES AND SUGAR-CANE

This is the sweetest chapter in the book. The pictures are enough to make one's mouth water and give one an appetite for Arabian dates. I do not suppose there is a boy or girl in England or America that has not eaten the fruit of the Arabian palm tree; but how many of you know the taste of sugar-cane?

In many parts of Arabia, especially at Busrah and along the river Tigris, you can see the sugar-cane sellers sit by the wayside and dispose of this Arabian stick-candy to the boys and girls in exchange for coppers. The woman in the picture has chosen the shelter of a date tree and beside the tall bundles of cane she has oranges for sale as well. The sugar-cane is cut into pieces and sold "by the knot"; that is, by the length of the stick from one knot to the next. It is not expensive and I have seen even the very poorest children suck their cane on the way home as happy as sugar can make them. The sugar-cane is a kind of grass but it grows to twice the height of a boy and is over two inches in circumference. The stems are smooth, shining and hard on the outside, but inside they are porous and the pores are full of sugar sap. The sugar-cane first came from India, but the Arabs spread its cultivation as far as Morocco and Sicily; so that it is no wonder that the word "sugar" itself comes from the Arabic. Yet it shows how ignorant the Arabs are to-day because, although they have sugar-cane, *their* sugar nearly all comes from Europe. They do not know how to manufacture it and therefore eat the sugar-cane raw.

WOMAN SELLING SUGAR-CANE.

Sweeter than sugar-cane and much more plentiful is the date. There is no place in all Arabia where you do not see the date palm growing, and seldom can you eat a meal in any part of the country but dates are part of the bill-of-fare. In fact thousands of people in Arabia have nothing but dates to eat from January to December! So plentiful are they that even donkeys and camels are fed on dates in some districts.

Many of the dates you buy in your own country come from Arabia. On the best kind of dates which come in wooden boxes you will find Muscat or Busrah stamped to show from what place they were shipped. There are very many kinds of dates in Arabia, and only a very few sorts are sent abroad. Some of them are too delicate to stand the long voyage and others are found only in small quantities. I do not think any of the dates that reach America equal those we pick from the palm tree ourselves here in Arabia—no more than dried apple rings taste as good as ripe juicy sweet apples from the orchard. When the dates ripen in September they are picked, sorted, and then packed in layers by the Arab women and boys who get paid for this work. Large steamships are loaded down with these boxes and many of them leave Busrah every year with no other cargo than dates.

DATES GROWING ON A DATE PALM.

The date tree is very beautiful. I think it is the most beautiful of all the palms. It is no wonder that a palm branch is the symbol of victory in the Bible and that the psalmist compares the life of a righteous man to a palm-tree! How straight and beautifully proportioned is the tall trunk of the tree. It is an evergreen and is always flourishing winter and summer. It is a lovely sight to see the huge clusters of ripening fruit, golden-yellow or reddish-brown, amid the bright green branches. Along the rivers in the north of Arabia, at Hassa and in Oman, date orchards stretch for miles and miles as far as you can see. Some of the Arabs have such large date gardens that they do not know the number of their trees. How do you suppose they climb the tree? The Arabs have no ladders and indeed it would be hard to make a ladder long enough to reach to the top of a tall palm tree. So they use a rope band which goes around the trunk of the tree and around their waist; it is shoved up little by little and the Arab puts his bare feet on the rough bark of the tree and so climbs up as easily as a monkey. The palm tree is perhaps the most useful tree in the world. Every part of it is used for something or other, and I do not see how Arabia could get along without palm trees. The fruit is prepared in many different ways for food. The date stones are used by the Arab children in playing checkers and other games on the smooth sand. They are also ground up into a coarse kind of meal and this is good cattle-food. The branches of the date tree are long and strong and thin just like a piece of rattan. From them the carpenters make beds, tables, chairs, cradles, bird-cages, reading-stands, boats, crates, kites and a dozen other useful things. The leaves are woven into baskets, mats, fans and string. From the bark excellent fibre makes rope of all sizes. Not a bit of the tree is wasted. Even the blossoms are used to make a kind of drink and the old musty fruit that cannot be eaten is made into date syrup or date vinegar.

In one of the pictures you see the fire wood market at Busrah. The long branches you see are sold for kindling wood and they make a splendid fire. The heavier parts of the tree are also used for fuel and the donkeys are loaded with these date knots and date sticks in baskets. It is a busy scene and, what with braying of donkeys and shouting of the wood-merchants, there is enough noise too.

FIRE WOOD MARKET, BUSRAH.

There is one more blessing that comes from the palm tree and which we have forgotten. That is shade. Arabia is a hot and dry country. The summer sun is much more piercing than in America and the summer is much longer. When you travel a long camel journey across the desert, oh how good it is to come to a grove of palm trees and rest! Such a place is called an *oasis* and underneath the palms there are always springs of water. I can well understand how happy the children of Israel were after their journey in the desert, when they came to Elim where "there were twelve wells of water and threescore and ten palm trees." In summer time many of the town Arabs leave their houses in the city and go to camp out in the date-gardens to enjoy the cool shades. The Arab poets have written many poems in praise of their favourite tree and fruit, but none of them are so funny as these lines which Campbell wrote from Algiers where the date tree also flourishes and with which we will end this chapter:

"Though my letter bears date as you view
From the land of the date-bearing palm
I will palm no more puns upon you."

VIII
THE SHEPHERD OF THE SEWING MACHINE

In the blue waters of the Persian Gulf there lies a coral island called Bahrein. At a few hundred yards to the northeast of it is a still smaller island shaped like a pack-saddle, where palm trees and white coral rock houses are reflected in the salt water at high tide. The little island town is called Moharrek, that is, the "Burning Place," because it is very hot there in summer. After sailing across in a boat one day, and wending our way through a dirty bazar full of flies and Arabs, we were directed to the house of the man called "The Shepherd of the Sewing Machine." His real name is Mohammed bin Sooltaan, but nobody knows him by any other name or title than *Räee el karkhan*, which literally means shepherd of the sewing machine. Let me tell you his story and how he got that queer name.

Years ago, as pilot on the native boats that sail from Bahrein to Bombay, Calcutta, Zanzibar and Jiddah, he had experience of a wider world than the little island where he was born. But the life was a hard one and his wages were small. Moreover, the coming of steamships up the Gulf took away the profit of the sailing craft, and so Mohammed fared from bad to worse. He loved an Arab lass with plaited, well-greased locks of hair and a pleasant face, but her father asked a larger dowry than he could ever pay.

An Arab young man must always pay a good price to the father of his sweetheart before he is allowed to marry her. But this Mohammed was too poor to pay the price asked. What a queer topsy-turvy custom it is for a man to buy his wife just as he buys a horse or a camel! The Arabs often ask how much a wife costs in America and wonder that we are not allowed by the Christian laws to send away our wives and marry others.

Mohammed could not stay at home so he once more went in a ship to Jiddah, the port to Mecca, where pilgrims from all the Moslem world exchange thought and money for bad bread and fanaticism. And yet even here the civilisation of the West tries to enter. Wandering through the bazars Mohammed for the first time saw a sewing machine, in the hands of an Indian tailor. A marvel to the sailor fisherman, indeed! Almost as great a miracle to him as the Koran. The more he looked the more he coveted, and he could not pass the place without reckoning up the possible profits of such an investment should he return with it to his native island. The result was that he forswore the sea and preferred another kind of wheel to that of the pilot. With many mutual *wallahs* the bargain was concluded and the machine reached Bahrein. It was the first on the islands, and all the sheikhs came to see its marvellous build and wonderful work. Mohammed has a Western head on Eastern shoulders, and there was not a screw or tension from treadle to shuttle, which he did not learn the use of. It is unnecessary to state at the cost of how many broken needles he became proficient. Amid cries of *ajeeb, ajeeb*, the first Arab shirt was stitched together, and even the youngsters on the street imitated the whirrr-clic-whirrr of the machine. As for Mohammed, he sewed on, and while his sandalled feet worked the treadle his mind worked out a problem something like this: Three long-shirts a day and an *abba*, at one *kran* per shirt and two for the abba, thirty-five krans per week, how long will it take to pay the dowry? An *abba* is a large over-garment worn by both men and women in Arabia. It is like a cape or overcoat but has no sleeves nor buttons. The Arabs in Bahrein put a great deal of pretty embroidery work on these garments and some of them are worth twenty or thirty dollars. But the sewing is done very cheaply. A kran is a Persian coin worth about ten cents; can you figure out how much Mohammed earned in a month?

The Shepherd of the Machine kept working away and when his hopes grew strong he sang at his work. In a few months he paid a visit to the Mullah (the Moslem priest or teacher), and that same night the Arab fiddles and drums rang out merry music around the palm-leaf hut of his beloved bride. But the music of the machine sounded still sweeter next morning. Daily bread, with rice, fish and dates, and on rare occasions even mutton, all came out of the machine. He loved the very iron of it and, as he told us, read a prayer over it every morning: *Bismillahi er rahman er raheem*. His was the only machine, and a small monopoly soon makes a capitalist. His palm branch hut was exchanged for a house of stone; and Allah blessed him greatly. No shepherd was ever more tender to his little lambs than Mohammed to the old machine.

When we entered the house on our first visit, there stood the machine! Not much the worse for wear, and with "*Pfaff*. C. Theodosius, Constantinople," still legible on the nickel-plate. But the old machine had found a rival. By its side stood another make of machine which looked strangely familiar to American eyes. It was while comparing the machines and drinking Arab coffee that we learned from Mohammed why he prized the old one as better. "Wallah," he said, "I would not sell it for many times its original price. There is blessing in it, and all I have comes from that machine, praise be to Allah." And so we sipped his cups and heard his story and ceased to wonder why he was called the Shepherd of the Sewing machine. The shepherd has a brother who wants to learn English and goes to Bombay every year—but that is another story.

There are many other sewing machines in Bahrein now, but Mohammed's was the first, and he introduced the others. Do you not think that he should be called the Christopher Columbus of Bahrein tailors?

IX
THE CHILDREN OF THE DESERT

About one-third of Topsy-turvy Land is desert and is the home of those Arabs that wander about from place to place and are called nomads or *Bedouin*. The word Bedouin means a desert-dweller. But you must not think that a desert is a flat country covered with a deep layer of sand without trees or shrubs. Oh no! There are such deserts in Arabia too, but the greater part of what is called desert is much more attractive and is only *desert* because it has no settled population and no villages. The soil is often very good and in springtime after the rains the whole of northern Arabia (where most of the nomads pitch their tents) is one vast prairie of wild flowers and green grass. The Arabs of the North are rich in flocks and herds. I am sure you can still find some who, like Job, have seven thousand sheep and three thousand camels and a very great household. They all live in tents and the tents of Arabia are not white and round like circus tents but jet black and square or oblong. You remember the Bible always speaks of the *black* tents of Kedar. They are black because they are woven from goat's hair which is used also for their garments and is almost as good a waterproof covering as india rubber. But when you have to spend a long hot day under such a roof as I have done you feel sorry for the Arabs that they have no better protection against the blazing sun. Everything is home-made and clumsy, but shall I tell you what I have found? There is no warmer hospitality in all the wide world than in these tents of Kedar. A few weeks ago I spent a Sabbath day resting by the way in one of these tents. The women brought water to cool my head; a great bowl of camel's milk was our drink even before they asked our errand; and at night they killed a fat kid and made a guest meal fit for an epicure.

The Arabs of the desert are more ignorant than those of the towns, but they are much kinder to strangers and treat their wives and children better. Their life is rather monotonous, but they enjoy it. Like the American Indians they prefer a tent to a house, and would rather change their home every day than settle down as farmers. When pasture fails for their flocks of sheep the chief gives notice and on the morrow the whole camp has moved away. Some tribes move every month and go for a long distance to find fresh pastures.

ARAB RIDERS WITH LANCES.

The Bedouin are divided into many tribes and clans. Some of them are friendly to each other but nearly all are at war with one another all the year round. Robbery and murder are very frequent. Every one goes armed with a long spear or with a gun, and many carry a war club and a sword as well. The largest Arab tribes and the wealthiest are the *Anaeze* and the *Shommar.* They have many fine horses. In the picture you see a group of them armed with their long spears. The spear of the leader is ornamented with a tuft of ostrich feathers; these spears are often over twelve feet long and have a sharp steel lance at the end. The Arabs are fond of games, especially galloping their horses and playing at war. They are very skillful riders and kind to their steeds; they do not spend much time in grooming them and they never use a whip and seldom a bit. Their bridle is like our halter strap, and the horse is so well trained that he needs no iron bit in his mouth.

One of the most interesting of all the Arab tribes is called *the Suleibi.* They are despised by all the other Arabs and seem to be of a different race. The women of this tribe are remarkable for their beauty and the men for their skill as blacksmiths and tinkers. They are always sought after to do the tinkering for the Arabs of all other tribes. They have no camels or horses but ride little donkeys and dress in gazelle skins. Some people think that this tribe is a remnant of the Christian population of Arabia; they have many curious beliefs and their name means, "Those-of-the-Cross." Perhaps some day a missionary will bring them back to a true knowledge of the Crucified One.

The nomads of Arabia are happy in springtime when there is enough grass for their flocks and the wells of the desert are full of water. But after the long summer drought there is often a great scarcity of food and even famine in many parts of Arabia. Then the nomads eat anything and drink the brackish water from the bottom of a mud pool with relish. In no country in the world is water so costly as in Arabia; nowhere is it so carefully used; an Arab never wastes a drop of water and looks surprised and pained when an European traveller rinses out a cup before drinking! The nomad Arabs eat locusts and wild honey as did John the Baptist. But I have also seen them eat the big lizards of the desert and the jerboas—a sort of desert rat. An Arab once stood amidst a circle of jewellers at Busrah and said: "On one occasion I had missed my way in the desert, and having no road-provision left, I had given myself up for lost, when all at once I found a bag of pearls. Never shall I forget that relish and delight so long as I mistook them for parched wheat; nor that bitterness and disappointment when I discovered that they were real pearls!" This story is told by a Persian poet and although it may not be true yet it teaches a lesson. To a hungry man a handful of wheat is better than all the pearls of the ocean.

PEARL MERCHANTS.

In his tent the Arab is very lazy. His only occupation is feeding his horses or milking his camels. The Arab girls go out to take care of the flocks while the wife performs all the domestic duties. She grinds wheat in the hand-mill; kneads and bakes bread; makes butter by shaking the milk in a leather bag; fetches water in a skin; works at the loom and is busy all the time. The Arab smokes his pipe, drinks coffee and talks to his friends; unless he is on the march or on a robbery excursion his life seems very lazy.

ARABIAN WATER-BOTTLE.

Scarcely any of the Bedouin can read, and they have neither schools nor mosques. The Bedouin sometimes say, "Mohammed's religion cannot have been intended for us; it demands washings, but we have no water; alms, but we have no money; pilgrimage to Mecca, but we are always wandering and God is everywhere." Yet outwardly they observe the Moslem religion of which they know so little. In our next chapter you will read how earnestly even the nomad children pray in the desert. And I believe God loves these sons of Ishmael and will yet bring them back to Abraham's faith. Don't you think so too?

X
NOORAH'S PRAYER

For many days the sailing craft from Bahrein had been unloading Indian wares at the port of Ojeir on the Hassa coast, and for many hours the busy throng of Bedouin drivers and merchants and onlookers were loading the caravan, emphasising their task or their impatience with great oaths, almost as guttural and angry as the noise of the camels. At length, with the pious cry of *Tawakalna*, "we have trusted in God," they are off.

A caravan is composed of companies, and while the whole host numbered seven hundred camels, with merchants and travellers and drivers, *our* company from Ojeir to Hofhoof counted only six. There was Salih and Nasir, a second son of the desert, both from Riad; a poor unfortunate lad with stumpy hands and feet, who limped about on rag shoes and seemed quite happy; there was Noorah and her sister, and lastly, the missionary.

But for the shuffling of the desert sand and the whack of a driving stick the caravan marched in silence. The sun shone full in our faces as it slowly sank in the west, its last rays coloured the clouds hanging over the lowlands of Hassa a bright red, and when it disappeared we heard the sheikhs of the companies, one after the other, call to prayer. Only a part of the caravan responded. The Turkish soldiers on horseback kept on their way; the most pious of the merchants had already urged their beasts ahead of the rest and had finished a duty that interfered with a speedy journey and the first choice of location at the night encampment; some excused themselves by quoting a Koran text, and others took no notice of the call. Not so the Bedouin child Noorah and her younger sister. They had trudged on foot four long hours, armed with sticks to urge on that lazy white camel, always loitering to snatch a bite of desert-thorn with his giant jaws. A short time before sunset I saw the two children mount the animal by climbing up its neck, as only Arabs can, but now, at call to prayer they devoutly slipped down. Hand in hand they ran ahead a short distance, shuffled aside some sand with their bare feet, rubbed some on their hands, (as do all pious Moslems in the absence of water), faced Mecca, and prayed.

As they did then, so at sunrise and at noon and at four o'clock and sunset and when the evening star disappeared—five times a day—they prayed. It is not true, as is generally supposed, that women in Moslem lands do not pray. Only at Mecca, as far as I know, of all Arabia, are they allowed a place in the *public mosques*, but at home a larger per cent. observe the times of prayer than do the men.

When Noorah had ended her prayer and resumed the task of belabouring the white camel, she turned to me with a question, *"Laish ma tesully anta?"*

which with Bedouin bluntness means, "*You*, why don't you pray?" The question set me musing half the night; not, I confess, about my own prayers, but about hers. Why did Noorah pray? What did Noorah pray? Did she understand that

Prayer is the burden of a sigh, the falling of a tear,The upward glancing of the eye when only God is near,

as well as the dead formalism of the mosque? How could I answer her question in a way that she might well understand? And if hers, too, was a sincere prayer, as I believe,—the prayer of an ignorant child of the desert,— did she pray words or thoughts? What do Noorah and her more than two million Bedouin sisters ask of God five times daily? Leaving out vain repetitions, this is what they say:

"In the name of God the Merciful, the Compassionate;
Praise be to God who the two worlds made;
Thee do we entreat and Thee do we supplicate;
Lead us in the way the straight,
The way of those whom Thou dost compassionate,
Not of those on whom is hate
Nor those that deviate. Amen."

It is the first chapter of the Koran and is used by Moslems as we use the Lord's Prayer. The words are very beautiful I think, don't you?

Whether Noorah understood what she asked I know not; but to me who saw and heard in the desert twilight, (as under like conditions to you), the prayer was full of pathos. The desert! where God is, and where but for His mercy and compassion death and solitude would reign alone; the desert, a world of its own kind, a sea of sand, with no life in it except the Living One, and over it only His canopy of stars—God of the two worlds! And to that God, than whom there is no other, and whom they ignorantly worship, these sons and daughters of outcast Ishmael bow their faces in the dust and five times daily entreat and supplicate to be led aright in the way of truth.

They ask to be directed into the *straight* way, but oh how crooked is the way of God which Mohammed taught in his book! Sadder still, what a crooked way it is that the Moslems walk! Impure words, lying lips, hands that steal and feet that run after cruelty—these are what children in Arabia possess. But I dare say that some of them are really sorry for their sins and when they pray like Noorah in the desert they want to have peace and pardon. Are they looking unconsciously perhaps for the footprints in the desert of One who said, "I am the Way, the Truth and the Life"?

Alas, Noorah and her many sisters (your sisters, too) have never seen His beauty nor heard of His love! They do not know that the "way of those whom Thou dost compassionate" is the new and living way through Christ's cross and death. They are ignorant of the awful word, "He that believeth not on the Son shall not see life, but the wrath of God abideth on him." Has God the Merciful then not heard Noorah's prayer? Will He not answer it? Is His mercy to these children of Abraham clean gone forever? How long they have waited and how many of the desert children are now sleeping in little desert graves! Do you not think God wants *you* to carry the gospel to them and send them teachers to learn the way of Jesus?

Think of Noorah's question, "*You*, why don't you pray?" Think of Christ's words, *"Go tell quickly."*

"ARABIA THE LOVED."

There's a land since long neglected,
There's a people still rejected,
But of truth and grace elected,
In His love for them.

Softer than their night wind's fleeting,
Richer than their starry tenting,
Stronger than their sands protecting,
Is His love for them.

To the host of Islam's leading,
To the slave in bondage bleeding,
To the desert dweller pleading,
Bring His love to them.

Through the promise on God's pages,
Through His work in history's stages,
Through the cross that crowns the ages,
Show His love to them.

With the prayer that still availeth
With the power that prevaileth,
With the love that never faileth,
Tell His love to them.

Till the desert's sons now aliens,

Till its tribes and their dominions,
Till Arabia's raptured millions,
Praise His love of them.

—J.G.L.

XI
PICTURES WITH WORDS ONLY

You already know many curious facts about the people of Topsy-turvy Land. Would you like to hear something about their language and their writing? The language of this land is very old, almost as old as its camels or its desert sands. The Moslems even go so far as to say that Adam and Eve spoke Arabic in Paradise and they say it is called the language of the angels. It is written from right to left just in the opposite way of this page of English writing. The Arabic alphabet has twenty-eight letters, all of which are considered consonants. There are marks put above and below the line to show the sounds of the vowels; just as we wrote the word *potato* in our first chapter.

Arabic grammar is much more difficult than English grammar, and even the boys who attend the big Arabic college of El Azhar in Cairo, Egypt, must find its study a bugbear. Just think of learning *fifteen* conjugations instead of the much smaller number in Latin or Greek! The books used in Moslem schools would look very crude and dull to you who learnt your A, B, C, from an illustrated primer perhaps with coloured pictures.

Strict Mohammedans do not allow their boys and girls to have pictures in their books, because they say all pictures are idols. And yet the love for beauty and the desire for ornament on the written or printed page was so strong with the Arabs that they began from the earliest times to use their alphabet to make arabesques. Arabesque is a big word and it really means an Arab picture. But these pictures of the Arabs (which you find on the arches of old mosques, in books and on tombstones) are ornaments or designs made out of the beautifully curved letters of the alphabet. The old Arab copyists and their sculptors wrote and carved the words of the Koran, or the names of God, etc., in all sorts of ways to make pictures *out of words only*, lest they break the law of their prophet. Here are two examples of how pictures can be made out of letters. You have all doubtless heard of a "wordless book"; and some of you have books without words and full of pictures. Here is a picture made out of the Arabic alphabet, and every curve and dot belongs to the words so curiously written. I copied them out of an Arabic treatise on penmanship, for you. The face is not at all pretty, and yet Moslem lads think it is very clever to bring this likeness of man out of the four names, *Allah, Mohammed, Ali* and *Hassan*. These words you notice are written twice, both to the left and to the right. What a disgrace to the holy name of God to put that of three Arabs with it in a monograph! It is very sad to hear some Moslems say that they trust in *these* people to intercede for them with God. If you have read what sinful lives these people led when they were the chief rulers in Arabia, you will almost agree with me in calling this first picture a Moslem idol.

DESIGNS MADE OUT OF ARABIC WRITING.

There are many Moslems in Bahrein who have hanging up in their rooms these monograms or designs. One favourite I have often seen contains only five names: *Allah, Mohammed, Ali, Hassan and Hussein.* The people who make so much of these descendants of Mohammed are called *Shiahs*; the other Moslems who think they are more orthodox are called *Sunnites.*

What do you think of our second picture? Is not the design very pretty for an embroidery pattern? The motto is written twice; once from the right and once *backward* from the left, the same as in the other picture. The words are taken from the Koran and are as true as they are beautiful. *Man yattawakil ala Allah fa hooa hasbahoo*; which means, "Whoever trusts in God will find Him sufficient." That surely contradicts the other picture, does it not? And yet they are both from the same copy-book. There are many contradictions in the religion of Mohammed. I only hope that when Christ's gospel has conquered Arabia, the name of Jesus will be written on every mosque and in every heart; then contradiction will give way to the truth, and whoever trusts in Christ will find Him sufficient.

Would it not be nice to make something pretty for use in the home or in the Sunday-school, and embroider the Arabic words on it? It would be a constant reminder of Arabia and of the beautiful motto—only an Arabic version of Paul's words, *Our sufficiency is of God.*

Our last illustration to close this chapter is an example of Arabic every-day penmanship. It was written in the mountains of Oman, and is a letter from a poor cripple asking for a copy of the Psalms and other books. It was sent to our brother Peter J. Zwemer a year before he died, when he was on a missionary journey in Oman.

بسم الله الرحمن الرحيم

الجناب .... الشيخ المحب الاكرم المكرم الاخ   ناصر علي   سلمك الله تعالى انشاء الله
خلفات
الله

سلام عليكم ورحمة الله وبركاته وبعد اعترفك سمعت عن الرجل الغرنيسي عند اكتب واريد
ان تشرك لي كتاب المستعمل البذر تجده واما الزهور واما الكتاب فيه شيء والقصص والجنات
باتستحسنه لي وعليكم جزيل السلام واخبك ناصر بيله سلم للناس على الخوه سعيد وعبده

ARABIC LETTER FROM A POOR CRIPPLE.

- 39 -

XII
THE QUEER PENNIES OF OMAN AND OF HASSA

If Jesus Himself, on one occasion, said, "Show me a penny," and preached a sermon from it, surely we may follow his example and learn something from these strange coins which you see in the pictures at the beginning and end of this chapter. The coin on this page comes from Oman, the home of the Arabian camel and one of its most fertile provinces. Perhaps some of the boys and girls can tell where Oman is and give its boundaries without looking in the geography, but I am sure none of you can read the inscription on the penny, and tell what it all means. Who is Fessul bin Turkee? What is an Imam? How much is one-quarter of an Anna? And when did this queer coin come fresh from the mint?

OMAN COIN.

Let us begin at the beginning. Fessul bin Turkee, the present ruler of Oman, lives in a large, tumble-down old castle in Muscat, and his big red flag waves over the town every Friday, the Mohammedan Sabbath. He is not much better nor worse than his father, Turkee, or than other rulers in Arabia, but he certainly is far more enterprising, and is generally liked by the Arabs of Muscat. He is not however in all respects a merciful ruler. When I visited Muscat a few years ago this petty king had a real lion's den, like Nebuchadnezzar, and the story goes that he sometimes used it in the same way to get rid of his enemies. He once had a steam-launch, and even put up an electric light on the top of his castle, but both of these modern improvements came to grief. He also started a small ice factory to supply his household with cold water when the thermometer rises to over one hundred degrees; but the expense was too great and so the project melted away likewise. His last venture is more successful, and ever since the ice factory added a P to its sign-board and became a "pice factory," copper coins have been plentiful in Oman. A *pice* is the Indian name for a small copper coin, and the Arabs borrowed the word, with many other words, from the Hindu traders. The Sultan has plenty of wives and horses and retainers; his castle is well-supplied with old cannon and modern rifles; huge coffee-pots pour out cheap hospitality every day; but withal I do not think he is very happy, for he is in debt and his power is not as extensive as it was once. Fessul's proper title is not Sultan, although he is often so called, but *Imam*, which signifies religious leader. It is the old title given to the political chiefs of Oman and Zanzibar.

The word means one "who stands before," and was first used as a title for the leader of prayer in the mosques. In Oman the religious chiefs soon took hold of politics, and so the title has a significance now in this part of Arabia that it never had elsewhere.

Let us get back to the penny. Its face (although being a Mohammedan coin it really has no human *face* because their religion forbids pictures) bears an English as well as an Arabic inscription. The opposite side only has the Sultan's name in Arabic. On the side that has the English words is the legend: "Struck at Muscat in the year 1315." Yet the penny is only three years old, for the Moslems begin to date their years from the *Hegira*, or flight of their prophet from Mecca to Medina. This took place in the year 622 A.D. But we must also remember that their year is several days shorter than ours, because they have lunar months all of equal length and only 360 days in a year.

How strange it is to read such an old date for such a recent year as 1899, since we count time from the birth of Christ! But you must remember that the False Prophet has had it all his own way in Arabia for thirteen hundred years, and that the missionaries in this country are very few indeed. Only for a very few years and in a very few places has Christ been preached.

Now, however, even this queer little penny can bear witness to the fact that the gospel has come to Oman. It is worth one-quarter of an anna; there are sixteen annas in a rupee, and a rupee is worth about thirty-three cents. Not a big value, is it? But for four of these coins the poorest boy in Muscat can buy a complete gospel of Matthew. The shopkeeper must take in a great many of them, for last year one thousand four hundred and thirty-three such gospels and other portions of the Bible were sold in this part of Arabia and paid for by these coppers.

Another interesting fact to notice is that part of the inscription on the coin is English. Coming events cast their shadows before. England's power in checking the cruel slave trade and rooting out piracy on the coasts of Arabia has made its influence felt. An English primer is sure to follow a penny with an English motto, and some day our mission will have a school at Muscat for Arab boys and girls, as well as for rescued slaves. Your American pennies and your prayers will help to bring it about. Moreover, do you not think that if they keep on buying gospels and reading them, Jesus Christ will some time be the true *Imam of Muscat and Oman*?

HASSA COINS.

The other coin is the only *old* coin that is at present current in Arabia, and I leave you to decide whether it is not the oddest and queerest penny you have ever seen. The first time I saw these queer blacksmith-nail coins was in 1893, when I made a visit to Hofhoof, the capital of the province of Hassa, in Eastern Arabia. The people used them, as we do pennies, for all small purchases, but I fear such a *pointed* coin must have been harder on their pockets than our round coins. It is called the *Taweelah*, or long-bit, and consists of a small copper-bar of about an inch in length, split at one end and with the fissure slightly opened. The coin has neither date nor motto, although one can yet occasionally find silver coins of like shape with the Arabic motto: *"Honour to the sober man, dishonour to the ambitious."* The coin, although it has no date, was undoubtedly made by one of the Carmathian rulers about the year 920 A.D. This was more than five hundred years before Columbus discovered America! The Carmathians were a very fanatical sect of Moslems. You remember reading in chapter three how they took the black stone from Mecca?

Well, these people had this province as the centre of their power and here they struck these peculiar coins. I have heard it said that they were so opposed to images and faces on money that their leader devised this long bar-like shape for his coins to prevent any one from making images on them!

At any rate the Carmathians were very brave warriors. When Abu Tahir, their first leader, attacked Bagdad with only 500 horsemen he was met by a messenger from the city saying that 30,000 soldiers were guarding the gates. "Yes," said Abu Tahir, "but among them all there are not three such as these." At the same instant he turned to three of his companions commanding one to plunge a dagger into his own breast, another to leap into the rushing Tigris river and the third to cast himself down a precipice. They obeyed without a murmur. "Relate," continued the general, "what you have just seen; before evening your leader shall be chained among my dogs." No wonder that with such absolute obedience, the Carmathians terrified all Arabia with their army.

As I handle their old coins and think of the past, I sometimes wonder how much Our Great Captain, Christ Jesus would accomplish had He soldiers equally obedient and brave as did the Carmathian general, in redeeming Arabia from its long darkness and bloodshed. It is nineteen hundred years ago that He commanded us: "Go ye into all the world and preach the gospel."

But even now there is no one preaching the gospel in Hassa nor in all the interior of Arabia. Why?

XIII
ARAB BABIES AND THEIR MOTHERS

An Arab baby is such a funny little creature! In Christian lands babies, as soon as possible, are given a warm bath and dressed with comfortable clothing. But in Arabia the babies are not washed for many days, only rubbed over with a brown powder and their tiny eyelids painted round with collyrium. They are wound up in a piece of calico and tied up with a string, just like a package of sugar. Their arms are fastened by the bandage so that they cannot possibly move them. The Arab mothers say that if the arms and legs of babies were left hanging loose the poor things would never sleep. A small, tight bonnet for the head completes the baby's wardrobe. A few blue beads or buttons are sewn on the front of this cap to keep off the evil-eye, for Moslem women all believe that if a stranger looks at a baby it may turn sick and die.

On the day when the baby is named a sacrifice is slain and eaten and silver offerings are given to the poor, equal to the weight of hair on the infant's head. The poor baby's hair is all shaved off to be weighed in the balance. Poor people who cannot afford this offering omit the custom. Charms are placed on the arms or around the neck of the child. A few verses from the Koran are written out and put in a leather or silver case and also tied around the arm or neck of the baby. If the child shows signs of illness the mother makes it swallow some of the Koran. That is, a portion is written out and the ink is washed off with water and this dirty water is taken by the patient. A prescription was sent to me once when I was ill by a Moslem *mullah*, or teacher, of this character and he was quite certain I would recover if I drank it. I am glad to say I got better without the ink medicine.

DATE-STICK CRADLE.

When the baby is forty days old and has received its name a new date-stick cradle is triumphantly brought home from the market and the new baby placed in it. And then Master or Miss Arab will get such a violent rocking that no Christian baby could stand. The ground is uneven, for there are no wooden floors in Arabia, and the rockers are nearly straight so that you can imagine it is not the pleasantest thing in the world to be rocked in an Arab cradle. In the picture you can see just what a date-stick cradle is like.

Arab babies cry a great deal; what with sand storms and flies and other insects they generally have sore eyes and apparently need strong treatment to make them quiet and give their mothers and sisters time to grind the wheat and churn the butter. Everything is made fresh each day in an Arab household. The rice must be cooked for the daily meal, the wheat ground for bread, and the milk put into the leather churn. These people have no ice chest, not even cupboards, many of them, so the coffee is freshly roasted and pounded in a mortar for breakfast. The flour is taken to the hand-mill and butter comes out of the churn every day fresh. Then the mother will have to draw the daily supply of water and wash the few clothes at the well. The better classes have their slaves to do the hard work but the Bedouin women and the poor have to do all the toil and never get a rest. Rich and poor are alike in not having any intellectual pleasures. Few can read and even those who can read, are able to read only the Koran and the Moslem traditions. The children have no primers or picture-books, and no Arab mother ever has a newspaper or a magazine. She has never heard of such things. Arab women do not know anything of the many interests and pleasures that occupy the time of women in Christian lands.

WOMEN GRINDING AT THE MILL.

Would you like to know how they make bread in Arabia? First the wheat is sifted and cleaned and then it is put into one of the hand-mills. It consists of an upper and nether millstone with a hole in the upper one and a wooden handle. Two women usually sit and grind because the stone is heavy and they love to talk while they work. One swings it half way and the other pulls it around. Then the coarse flour is taken out and put into a bowl with water and salt and mixed to the right consistency. A piece of this dough is then taken between the hands and gradually beaten until it is about the thickness of a book cover and twelve inches in diameter—a round, flat cake of dough. The oven is usually under ground and is shaped like a large jar with the mouth above the ground a little. A fire is built *inside* the oven and when the sides of the oven are quite hot the fire is allowed to die out. Then the large pan cakes of bread are deftly clapped on to the side of the oven until the space is covered and one by one the cakes are taken out when done. In some houses they have a shallow oval pan which is placed over an open fire and on this the cakes are baked. The pan is put on the fire upside down, so even here we are again in Topsy-turvy Land. Twenty or thirty of these flat loaves are baked at one time, for a hungry Arab can eat five or six at one meal.

BEDOUIN WOMEN EATING THEIR BREAKFAST.

Now the men come in to eat the food that the housewife has prepared. With a short prayer called *bismillah* they begin and then shove the rice and meat or the bread and gravy into their mouths as fast as they can. Whatever is left when the men get through is for the women. You can see a group of Arab women in the picture eating their meal from one common dish in front of their tent. They use their hands instead of spoons or forks but get along very well and always wash before and after their simple meal.

Now the women always have to wait on their husbands and eat by themselves. When things get right side up in this dark land we hope to see the whole family sitting down together and taking their meal with joy and thanksgiving.

XIV
BOAT-BUILDERS AND CARPENTERS

Sinbad the sailor died long ago but the sea he sailed is still called the Persian Gulf and is just as full of curious islands as it was in his time. The boats are also just like Sinbad's and the sailors sing the same songs, I think, for there are very few changes in the almost changeless East. The Bahrein harbour-boat is built on the islands, out of timber from India and masts from Ceylon. But the sailcloth and the ropes are made on this our island home. All boats of this kind carry a good lot of passengers, draw very little water and are fast sailing craft; so that even the American boy whose father owns a yacht would not speak with contempt of one of these boats. In fact I have heard English sea captains who had drunk salt water for years say that they never saw better harbour boats in a storm than these of Bahrein.

CARGO BOATS, BAHREIN.

In another kind of boat the pearl-divers of the Gulf go out to their hard toil and costly labour. One of them costs about four hundred *rupees*, that is about one hundred and thirty dollars. You do not think that is dear, do you, for a boat that holds a crew of twenty? But the cost of diving for pearls is not in the boat or the apparatus; it costs lives. Many of the divers are eaten by sharks before they return with the year's pearl harvest; others lose limbs and health. I wish you could see the odd shaped oars the Arabs use in these boats. They consist of a round pole with a sort of barrel-head or spoon shaped board tied to one end. The boat builders always use twine and rope rather than nails or screws to put their boats together. The boys of Bahrein can make beautiful sailing boats to play with out of bits of date-stick and strings.

RIVER BOAT, BUSRAH.

Each fishing boat has a sort of figure-head and this is generally covered with the skin of a sheep or goat. This animal is sacrificed on the day when the boat is first launched, just as we give the boat a name and put flags on it. It is a very old custom to offer a blood sacrifice when a boat is first put into the water.

Not only in the villages on the coasts of the Red Sea and the Persian Gulf are there boat builders and sailors; Arabia has two large rivers that help to make its northern boundary and they are highways of traffic.

Our picture shows a river boat on the canal at Busrah. It goes the long journey from Busrah to Bagdad over five hundred miles or even to Hillah and the other towns on the Euphrates river. This kind of boat has a cabin in the bow and can carry a large cargo of wheat or wool. It sails by all the interesting country which was once the home of Abraham and is still called Mesopotamia.

The largest boats used by the Arabs are called *dhows* or *buggalows*. You will hear something more about these boats in the chapter on the slave trade.

The carpenters of Arabia, like the boat builders, work in a very old-fashioned way. But they are much less skillful in their work. You often see well-built boats but never a well-made door or a window that shuts properly. Perhaps the fault is with their tools and perhaps they are not as skillful as they once were in using them.

The Arab carpenter uses no bench or vise; he squats upon the ground in the shade of some old building or tree and carries all his tools in a small basket with him. He has four hands instead of the two hands of an American carpenter, for his feet are bare and he can work as well with his toes as you can with your fingers. It is wonderful to see how an Arab carpenter can hold a board with his toes while his hands are busy sawing or planing it!

I never see one of these carpenters using his toes so cleverly without thinking that we who wear shoes and stockings and only use our feet for walking have lost one of the powers that the Arabs still possess. A carpenter's handsome handiwork in Arabia should be called his *toe*some *toey*-work; don't you think so? In the picture at the end of this chapter you see an Arab carpenter's tools. His saw is exactly opposite to an ordinary saw as the teeth all point the wrong way! But you know he *pulls* the tool so it is all right. The plane has four handles instead of one. The gimlet is like ours but instead of a brace and bit to make holes, the Arab uses a fiddle-string stretched on a bow which he twists once or twice around his borer, or auger-bit. Then he fiddles away until he has made a hole.

SAWING A BEAM.

It is very strange to see two Arab carpenters sawing a beam as you find them in the picture.

Time is not valuable in the East because the days are long and life is easy and the people are never in a hurry. Never do anything to-day that can be done to-morrow is their motto. So they spend a half hour in fixing the beam on a tripod; then they pull and push and push and pull the great clumsy saw blade up and down and in an hour or so the beam is cut in two. What would such carpenters say if they were to visit an American sawmill and see the gang-saw cut six boards out of a log at once just as easy as your mother cuts a cheese? Arabia and its carpenters are very far behind us in civilisation. The whole country is in need of schools and industrial missions so that the Arab boys may learn to handle tools and make furniture and build houses.

AN ARAB CARPENTER'S TOOLS.

In America there is hardly a boy living but he can drive a nail and saw off a board and put up a shelf. In Arabia only carpenters' sons can do these things; the ordinary boy does not even know how to use a jack-knife; he never had one. A short definition of Arabia would be "a land without tools." Ritter, the great geographer, calls Arabia "the anti-industrial centre of the world," which is only the same definition in other words.

XV
ARABIC PROVERBS AND ARABIC HUMOUR

The people of Topsy-turvy Land, like all orientals, are very fond of proverbs and short, bright sayings. You know that even to-day there are men who go about in the coffee shops of Arabia to tell stories, just as you have read in the Arabian Nights. Some of their stories are very interesting and some of their proverbs are wise. Others are not interesting and many of their stories are too bad to repeat. Even some of their proverbs bear the mark of their topsy-turvy religion and are only half true. Judge them for yourself. Here are fifty examples; which do you think is the best proverb among them? Are they all good?

- First seek your neighbour, then build your house.

- First get a companion, then go on the road.

- Whoever dies in a strange land, dies a martyr.

- When the judge is oppressive, the very air is, too. Don't cut your head off with your tongue.

- Keep your dog hungry and he will follow you.

- Leave off sin, then ask forgiveness.

- Every horse knows its rider.

- Talk is feminine, but a good answer is masculine.

- With little food a bed tastes good.

- A trotting dog is better than a sleeping lion.

- Every girl is beautiful in her father's eyes.

- His tongue is sweeter than dates but his hands are as hard as sticks.

- There is no perfume after the wedding.

- Clouds do not fear the barking of dogs.

- A bird catches a bird.

- Poverty is the mother of deceptions.

- The fruit of haste is repentance.

- That man is like the *Kaaba*; he goes nowhere but every one comes to him.

- The tongue of a fool is the key to his destruction.

- The needle clothes others but is itself naked.

- If the owl were game to eat, the gunner would not have passed by the ruined castle.

- Happy is the man whose enemy is wise.

- Time is stingy of honour.

- The best generosity is quick.

- If your neighbour is honey, don't lick him all up.

- If you don't know a man's parents look at his appearance.

- What a strange world if all wool were red!

- Fall but don't bawl.

- Your enemy will love you when the ass becomes a doctor.

- Wait, donkey, till the grass grows.

- A loaned garment is not warm.

- He is a hard man; his name is Rock, son of a Cliff.

- The oppression of a cat is better than the justice of a rat.

- While I was fishing, I was caught.

- A blacksmith came to shoe the Pasha's horse and a frog in the pond stuck out her foot too.

- One nettle seed will ruin a garden.

- Who speaks the whole truth will get a broken head.

- What's the good of a house without food?

- Ask experience but don't neglect the doctor.

- She wears seven veils but has no modesty.

- He fasted a year and breakfasted on an onion.

- A false friend is an open enemy.

- They gave me no food, but the smoke from their kitchen blinded me.

- When the lion is away, the hyenas play.

- They said to the blind man, throw away your stick; he replied, why desert an old friend?

- Haste is of the devil; deliberation, of God.

- They put the dog's tail in the press forty years, and when it came out it still had a curl.

- Lucky days do not come in a bunch.

- Look for a thing where you lost it.

Some of these resemble our own proverbs and others may perplex you at first. Of course they are all better in Arabic than in the translation. The people of Arabia seldom or never engage in practical jokes, but they are often very witty in their remarks. The Caliph Mansur once met an Arab on the desert and said to him: "Give thanks to God who has caused the plague to cease that ravaged thy country."

"God is too good," the Arab answered, "to punish us with two such scourges at the same time as the plague and thy government."

An Arab poet sent his book to a famous author. "Dost thou want fame?" said the latter, "then hang thy book up in the market-place where all can see it."

"But how will they know the author?"

"Why, just hang yourself close to the book!"

Here is another story that is told about a Moslem preacher. One Friday when the people were gathered in the mosque to pray and to hear the sermon, he got up in the pulpit and asked the audience if they knew what he intended to preach about.

"No," they replied.

"Well, then, I shall not tell you," and he stepped down. The next Friday he asked the same question, and now, taught by experience, they answered:

"Yes, we know."

"Well, then, I need not tell you," and again he stepped down.

The third Friday when the same question was put, the people said, "Some of us know and some don't know."

"In that case," said the preacher-wag, "let those of you who know tell those that don't know." And again there was no sermon.

And now to close this chapter here is a very topsy-turvy story with a puzzle in it:

The Arabs relate that when the prophet Jonah fled from Joppa to Tarshish, there were thirty passengers, all told, in the ship. The storm grew very fierce, and out of fear, the captain determined to throw half the crew overboard, that is, fifteen men. But he knew that fifteen of the thirty were true believers, and fifteen were infidels, and among them, Jonah also. To avoid suspicion and accomplish his purpose he put the thirty men all in a row in such a way that by counting out every ninth man, the believers alone remained and the unbelievers were all of them one by one cast into the sea.

This is the way he arranged them; every *dot* stands for an *unbeliever*, and the strokes for believers—thirty altogether.

IIII • • • • •II•III•I••II • • •I••II•

PUZZLE OF THE THIRTY MEN.

You begin to count from the left, as the captain did, and if you mark out every ninth man you can keep on counting out the ninth men until only upright strokes are left.

From your knowledge of arithmetic, can you tell me the reason of this puzzle?

The Arabs remember the puzzle by some verses in which every dotted letter stands for an unbeliever and those that have no dots stand for Moslems.

You see that even the story of Jonah and the whale is topsy-turvy out in Arabia!

XVI
GOLD, FRANKINCENSE AND MYRRH

In olden times Arabia was a much more important country than it is to-day. Before there were large seagoing ships, all the trade between India, Persia, even China, on the east, and Egypt on the west, was carried on camels. The caravans at that time used to cross Arabia in all directions, and the men who drove these camel-trains grew wealthy, as railroad magnates do to-day. We read about this early traffic on these highways of the desert in the Old Testament as well as in the old Greek histories. The province of Yemen was celebrated for its wealth and civilisation as early as the time of Solomon. It was then called Sheba and the old capital was called Marib, a little northeast of the present city of Sanaa. There are still many extensive ruins and inscriptions which testify to the height of their civilisation. We read of one of the queens of Sheba (the Arabs say she was named *Bilkis*) who came to prove Solomon with hard questions. She came with a large caravan of camels bearing spices and gold in abundance; her present to Solomon consisted of "an hundred and twenty talents of gold, and of spices great abundance, and precious stones." Gold is no longer found in Arabia but it was undoubtedly once very plentiful there. All the old writers speak of Arabia as a-gold country. One of the Greek geographers speaks of a stream in which large nuggets of gold were found. Some people think Ophir was in Arabia. However that may be, the traveller Burton explored the northwestern part of the peninsula and found old mines and even traces of gold dust. If Job lived in the land of Midian we can well understand how he could describe mining operations so well as he does in the twenty-eighth chapter of his book.

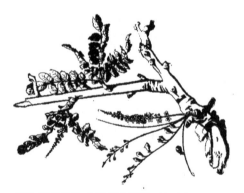

BRANCH OF INCENSE TREE.

Frankincense and myrrh were also carried across Arabia by the caravans, and both of these precious gums came from Arabia itself and are still found there. One of the oldest articles of commerce was incense. The gum was used in sacrifices and in all the heathen temple worship as well as by the Jews in their worship. One thousand talents' weight of frankincense was brought every year to Darius, the Persian king, as tribute from Arabia. The present incense country is southern Arabia, especially Hadramaŭt. Here the incense tree (of which you see a small branch in the picture) grows. The young trees are cut with a knife, and from the incisions made in the bark a milk-like juice comes out. When it has had time to harden, the large clear globules are scraped off into baskets and the inferior kind that has run down the bark is collected separately. It is shipped from Arabia to Bombay or goes out from Aden and still commands a good price. In some Roman Catholic churches this incense is burnt every Sunday and if you will go to a large druggist he may be able to show you pieces of Arabian incense.

Myrrh and frankincense are frequently mentioned together. Both are sweet-smelling gums and both came originally from Arabia. According to a Greek legend, Myrrha was the daughter of one of the kings of Cyprus who angered her father and when he attempted to stab her, fled to Arabia. Here she was changed into a tree called myrrh! A few of these trees are still found in Yemen, but myrrh is not at all as plentiful as it once was in Arabia. It is a low, thorny, ragged-looking tree with bright green leaves. The gum exudes from cracks in the bark near the root of the plant. When dry it is of a rich brown colour and has a bitter taste. The word "myrrh" in Arabic means bitter, and I think that is the origin of the name given to the tree and not the foolish story of the Greek mythology. You must look up all the references in the Bible to myrrh. I wonder whether the myrrh which Nicodemus used to embalm the body of our Saviour for His burial came from Arabia? In Matthew's gospel we read of the wise men who came from the East to worship Jesus. "And when they had opened their treasures they presented unto Him gifts; gold and frankincense and myrrh." Do you not think that these wise men came from Arabia, even as the queen of Sheba did, to see the king of the Jews? Perhaps Isaiah prophesied of their coming when he wrote concerning Arabia: "The multitude of camels shall cover thee the dromedaries of Midian and Ephah; all they from Sheba shall come: they shall bring gold and incense; and they shall shew forth the praises of the Lord." At any rate we are quite sure that the frankincense they brought came from Arabia. There is a great deal in the Bible about this country and there are many beautiful promises for the redemption of its people. Arabs were present at Pentecost and the first missionary to Arabia was the Apostle Paul. God has not forgotten His promises and we must all pray that soon they may be fulfilled. No one has yet been to tell the children of Hadramaŭt, who gather the incense-gum, the story of Jesus' birth and of His death on the cross. There is not a single missionary in all that country; no one has been to tell the news that the Babe of Bethlehem is the King of Glory.

"Thou who in a manger
Once hast lowly lain,
Who dost now in glory
O'er all kingdoms reign,
Gather in the heathen
Who in lands afar
Ne'er have see the brightness
Of Thy guiding star."

XVII
SLAVES AND SLAVE TRADERS

The Arabs who in past ages were the merchants of the Orient in gold, frankincense and myrrh, both then and now traded in slaves also. And the cruel trade is not yet ended. Would you like to hear about some boys who have darker skins than yours, and darker hearts, because they do not know the Lord Jesus as their own Saviour? Well, these poor little boys were stolen from their mothers and fathers by wicked men called Arabs, who go from Arabia to Africa in boats to steal boys and girls and bring them here to sell them. Each boy is sold for nearly ten pounds ($50). These men know it is wrong in their hearts, but you see what a lot of money they make! What does St. Paul say? "The *love* of money is the root of all evil." And then the religion of the Arab permits him to do this work of stealing and selling boys and girls.

One night about two or three years ago, just as the sun was setting, some little black boys were playing and fishing near the water on the coast of Zanzibar, in East Africa; a man came up to them and offered them some dates. Little black *and white* boys are always ready to eat, are they not? These boys took the dates and while they were eating, the man threw a cloth over their heads and carried them off to a boat standing near. The Arabs caught a great many in this way, and when the boat had as many as it could carry they moved away and began to travel towards Arabia. The poor children were kept in the bottom of the boat, all huddled together, and given very little to eat and drink. Sometimes the sea was rough and they were sick, so altogether their voyage in an open boat was not a pleasant one. But "Some One" was taking notice of these children and He was going to deliver them. Do *you* know who was watching over them? After many days at sea the boat came near Muscat. A servant of the British Consul saw the boat and knew there were slaves in it. Then the Consul got ready in a small boat and went after the big one. They had to follow nearly all night and at last overtook the slave-dhow. The Consul pulled alongside in a Bedden (native boat) and demanded the firearms of the Arabs. Then he bound them and put his own sailors on board, and brought the precious cargo of souls into Muscat harbour.

SLAVE GIRL IN ARABIA.

The owner of the slave-dhow was sent to prison, and the boys and girls were given away to Christian people to train, the missionary in Muscat getting the largest share.

This was the origin of the rescued-slave school at Muscat. Other slaves are caught from time to time and liberated. Sometimes they are sent to Bombay or other places in India; a large number were once liberated at Aden and are now in a school at Lovedale in Africa. When these poor slave children first come from the slave ships they are very ignorant and almost like wild animals. They need to learn everything, and even their language is of little use to them, as they need to learn Arabic before they can get along in Arabia. The Muscat boys first learned English from the missionary, but it was not easy for them.

They only knew a few words when I first went to Muscat. For instance, they called all lights, such as lamps, candles, etc., *fire*. Well, one night we were sitting on the verandah with the lamp, reading, and Suliman came and said *"big fire!"* We jumped up and said "where?" Looking all around we could not see a sign of fire. Then he said, "big fire on table." We ran into the dining-room—still no fire. Suliman then pointed to the lamp and said again "big fire"; so we learned by that time he wanted the lamp for the table, as dinner was ready.

LIBERATED SLAVES AT BAHREIN.

Would you like to hear how a day was spent in this Muscat school when the boys were beginning to learn? Now the boys are all big and have scattered; they are working as servants in different places and some are learning a trade. But here is a description of the early days of their training: "We are up before dawn almost, and yet the boys are up before us, and have taken in their mats (beds), and are splashing about in the big cement bath in the yard. They do not use towels; the sun soon dries the skin, and then they dress with one article only, a *wazeera*, a piece of cloth. After the bath they clean up the schoolroom, sweep the yard; then they eat bread and dates and drink water. When the meal is finished all the boys wash their hands and put on their coats to come up-stairs. See how nicely they march forward, two and two, just like the animals going into Noah's Ark. They *halt* in front of the harmonium 'single file'—'face about'—'toes to line!' Now we are ready for prayers. Look, boys and girls, how quietly these black boys stand; now we are going to sing:' 'Jesus loves me, this I know.' They love the singing, and all make as much noise as possible. Singing finished, we read a short passage of Scripture, and tell very simply how Jesus loved them and died for them. They are beginning to learn about God and who the Lord Jesus is. One morning I held up the Bible and asked them, 'What is this?'

"They answered, 'God's Book.'

"'And what do we read about in God's Book?'

"They all answered, 'The Lord is my shepherd I shall not want.' I had been teaching them this Psalm, but I did not know how well they knew it; it was a nice answer, do not you think so? After the scripture lesson we kneel and pray, all the boys repeating, 'O God, wash me from all my sins in the blood of my Saviour, and I shall be whiter than snow; give me Thy Holy Spirit, for Jesus' sake. Amen.' Will you ask God to make the boys pray this prayer from their hearts? You see they are only just beginning to learn about God. Before they came to us they were quite heathen. Prayer ended we all march into another room,—you may come too, and begin lessons. The big boys are learning sentences now; the little ones are still at A, B, C, 1, 2, 3. At the end of two hours of spelling, reading and writing, a little simple drill and the morning school is ended. Some of the boys help prepare their fish and rice for dinner, and others make baskets. At three o'clock all march up again for sewing. And let me tell you a secret; the smallest boy of all sews the neatest. After this the boys get ready to go for a bath in the sea, or for a walk. When we return we have evening prayers, and then the boys eat their supper of rice and fish, take their mats into the garden and go to sleep."

That was the way in which eighteen rescued slave boys began to live a life with more light, and therefore also more responsibility than their former life as savage children in Africa.

But what of the thousands who are *not* rescued, but are taken to places along the coast of Arabia and sold? Their lot is miserable. In Mecca there is a slave market where boys and girls are sold to the highest bidder. At Sur, in South Arabia, there are still many Arabs who make money by buying and selling poor negro children. Only last month a little negro lad called "Diamond" told me how he had been captured and sold to a merchant in Persia. I am very glad that I can tell you that the little lad escaped to a British ship and is now free.

A writer who travelled in the Red Sea says that he passed hundreds of slave-dhows. What a lot of misery that means; not only misery to the parents of these stolen children in Africa, but to the children themselves. There may be many slaves in Arabia who get enough to eat and have good clothing to wear, but they always remain slaves at the best, and are taught a false religion by their masters. I think dearly all of them were happier at home in Africa than in dark Arabia.

It is hard to love the cruel slave trader, is it not? Yet Jesus told us to "love our enemies." The way to root out the slave trade is to evangelise the slave trader. The entire west coast of Arabia has not a single missionary; no wonder that here the slave trade is carried on without hindrance! Will you not pray for western Arabia, and also for the Arab slave dealers that God may soften their hearts and make them stop their bad work? And will not all the girls pray for their enslaved black sisters in Arabia, whose lot is very miserable?

XVIII
ABOUT SOME LITTLE MISSIONARIES

Some little missionaries came to Arabia a few years before any of the American missionaries did, and have been coming ever since. Most of them were born in a country not far from Arabia, and yet only one of them visited Arabia before Mohammed was born. Although they never write reports of their work in the papers, yet I have seen a few splendid little accounts of their work written on tablets of flesh with tears for ink. It is just because their work is done so much in secret and in out-of-the-way places, that they are generally overlooked and often underestimated. They receive only bare support and no salary, and get along in the most self-denying way by fasting and living all together, packed like herring in a dark, close room, except when they go out into the sunshine on their journeys.

Most of them came out in the steerage of the big ships from London, but none of them were seasick at all throughout the entire voyage. They do not go about two and two unless it is that one of the old ones goes hand in hand with a younger brother for support. Generally a score or more travel together. They never complain of being tired or discouraged, and never get fever or cholera, although I have talked and slept with them at Bahrein when I had fever myself. Never yet has one of them died on a sick-bed, although they often hide away and disappear for months. On one or two occasions I have heard of a small company of them being burned at the stake, but I was told that not a groan escaped from their lips, nor were their companions frightened the least bit. With my own eyes I have seen one or two of them torn asunder and trampled upon by those who hate Jesus Christ and His kingdom and His little missionaries. Yet the only sound to be heard was the blasphemies of their persecutors, who could not answer them in any other way.

It is very strange indeed, that when once one or two of them get acclimatised and learn the language, they are bound to their work by so many tiny cords of love that they seldom fall apart from their work or fall out one with the other. There are more than sixty different names and ages among them, and yet they all have one family accent. Some of them are medical missionaries and can soothe and heal even broken hearts and prevent broken heads. There are two ladies among them, but they seldom go about alone, and, especially in Arabia, the men do most of the preaching. Most of them are evangelists or apostles and teachers. And their enterprise and push! why one of them told me the other day that he wanted *"to preach the gospel in the regions beyond"* Mecca, and that even there *"every knee should bow to Jesus."* Why, you begin to see them everywhere in the Persian Gulf and around Muscat and Aden. Last year a few of them went to Jiddah with the pilgrims. They dress very plainly, but often in bright Oriental colours (one just came in all in green); on one or two occasions I have seen them wear gold when visiting a rich man, but there was no pride about them, and they put on no airs in their talk.

MISSION HOUSE AT BUSRAH.

How many are there of these little missionaries, do you ask? Over three thousand eight hundred and forty visited and left the three stations of the Arabian Mission in the Persian Gulf last year. But, as I told you, they are *so* modest that only a score of them perhaps sent in any account of their work, and that even was sent through a third party by word of mouth. I have heard it whispered that a faithful record of all their journeys and speeches is kept, but that these are put on file to be published all at once on a certain great day, when missionaries all get their permanent discharge. What a quiet, patient, faithful, loving body of workers they are. Even when it is very, very hot, and after a hard day's work, they never get out of temper as other missionaries sometimes do when in hot discussion with a bigoted Moslem. And yet how plainly they tell the truth—they do not even fear a Turkish Pasha; but that is because they have very cunningly all obtained a Turkish passport and a permit to preach anywhere unmolested.

Of course, you have guessed my riddle, or else you will want to know what these missionaries cost and why we do not employ more of them; and who sent them out, and to what Board they are responsible; and who buys them new clothes of leather and cloth; and what happens to them when their backs are bent with age and their faces furrowed with care, and when only they themselves can read their title clear?

I think no one will have to help you guess my riddle or tell you that the four missionaries who go about the most are Matthew, Mark, Luke and John, and that the two ladies are Esther and Ruth. Now you have guessed that the Little Missionaries are the Books of the Bible. Do you know how many there are?

How many in the Old Testament? How many in the New Testament? Perhaps some of you know the names of *all* the sixty-six! But it is not enough to know the names of these Books that we have called Little Missionaries. We must know what is in them, we must know the message they bear to this sinful and troubled world. And we must all do our part to send out this blessed message of peace, comfort, and eternal life. It may not be your work to go to Arabia, but yet you have a work to do of one kind or another for Arabia. The Bible must be sent there. And now may I ask all the boys and girls who read this to pray for the Little Missionaries? Pray that they may go ahead and prepare the way of the Lord all over this dark peninsula, from the palm groves of Busrah to the harbour of Aden, and from the sea of Oman to the unholy cities,—Mecca and Medina.

"Jesus, tender Shepherd
Thou hast other sheep
Far away from shelter
Where dark shadows creep.
Seeking Saviour, bring them home
That they may no longer roam.

"Jesus, tender Shepherd
While Thou leadest me,
As Thy little helper
Faithful may I be.
Seeking others far and wide
Drawing lost ones to Thy side."

XIX
TURNING THE WORLD UPSIDE DOWN

About eighteen hundred and fifty years ago two missionaries came to a town in Greece, called Thessalonica, and began to preach. They did nobody any harm and only talked about the love of Jesus Christ for sinners. A great number of people believed and attended their meetings. Some of the noble and wealthy women of the town also became Christians and for about three weeks the preaching went on unhindered. However, as soon as the enemies of the gospel saw that Paul and Silas were meeting with success they did their best to stir up trouble. A mob collected and with a great deal of noise and shouting pulled some of the new believers through the streets, crying: *"They that have turned the world upside down are come hither also!"* Just as it was in Thessalonica so it has been in every place where the gospel has been preached. The word of God does turn the world upside down. The gospel is powerful and its effect is often at first to stir up the envy and hatred of men who love not God. When the heathen are worshipping idols and enjoying sinful pleasures they like to be let alone. A thief does not like the policeman's lantern. Those who do dark things hate the light. The Moslem's idea of right and wrong is so crooked that he does not like to have it exposed.

THE SULTAN'S SOLDIERS.

Supposing there was a country where all the people wore their garments wrong side out because they knew no better, and then some one came wearing his clothes properly and trying to teach these ignorant people, would they not think *him* mad and say why do *you* not turn your coat inside out?

That is the very way Moslems regard the missionary. They often tell us, "You are so good and kind why don't you accept the true religion and become a believer?" You must not think that the heathen or the Mohammedans are anxious to hear the gospel. They do not know of its value and so do not know what they miss. When they hear that the gospel demands a holy life and forbids all swearing and lying and uncleanness, they think such a religion too difficult and prefer their own. All their topsy-turvy ways and thoughts seem perfectly correct to themselves until God's Spirit enlightens them.

It is no wonder therefore that there is always opposition and trouble when missionaries (even such quiet *little* missionaries as we read about), come to a village. When you want to put a thing straight that is upside down there is sure to be an overturning. The farmer is not sorry because his rude plow breaks the hard soil and bruises the weeds and turns all the greensward under. Oh no; he does that to make some better green grow. Wait three months and you will see the whole field covered with a waving harvest of wheat. Ploughing is pretty rough work on weeds. Opening a new mission station is pretty rough, I admit, on a false religion. And the wise men cannot help knowing this and so they repeat the words of the old Greeks when they see a missionary settle down in their village: "Those that have turned the world upside down are come hither also ... saying that there is another King, *Jesus*."

The king of all hearts in the Mohammedan world is their prophet Mohammed. They love his name and imitate his acts to the least particular. Much more faithfully, I fear, than we imitate Jesus, our example. The great question in Arabia is whether Mohammed or Jesus is to rule the country. Mohammed has had it very much his own way for thirteen hundred years, but now his dominion is being disputed. God's providence is working in many ways to help His gospel. I sometimes think that we might call His providence the plow and His gospel the good seed. For example, what a strange thing it is for the Arabs to find Christian governments interfering with their slave trade. Does not the Koran approve of slave holders and did not Mohammed buy and sell slaves? And then when the big merchant ships come to the coasts of Arabia and the ignorant Arabs learn of other lands and peoples and civilisation they cannot help losing some of their pride and prejudice. They compare the government of England in Aden with that of the Turks in Sanaa and then—well they feel like turning the world upside down themselves!

The Mohammedan religion has such a strong hold in Arabia that it will not be overcome in one day or by one battle. We must expect a long and hard fight. Before Topsy-turvy Land becomes a Christian land there will be martyrs in Arabia. Every Moslem who accepts Christ does so at his peril, and yet there are those who dare to confess Christ before men. When you read in mission reports of troubles and opposition, of burning up books, imprisoning colporteurs and expelling missionaries you must not think that the gospel is being defeated. It is conquering. What we see under such circumstances is only the dust in the wake of the ploughman. God is turning the world upside down that it may be right side up when Jesus comes. He that plougheth should plough in hope. We may not be able to see a harvest yet in this country but, furrow after furrow, the soil is getting ready for the seed.

Don't some of you want to come and do a day's ploughing for the King? There are some splendid stretches of virgin prairie yet untouched between Bahrein and Mecca.

XX
TURNING THE WORLD DOWNSIDE UP

The story of mission work in Arabia is not very long, but it is full of interest. From the day when Mohammed proclaimed himself an apostle in Mecca until about sixteen years ago when Ion Keith Falconer came to Aden as a missionary, all of Topsy-turvy Land lay in darkness as regards the gospel. For thirteen hundred years Mohammed had it all his own way in Arabia. Now his dominion over the hearts of men, is in dispute, and there is no doubt that the final, full victory will rest with Jesus the Son of God, the Saviour of the world.

Would you like to hear something, before we close this book about the missions that are now working in this country? There are *three* missions. The missionaries of the Church of England began work in Bagdad about the year 1882. Bagdad is not at all a small town. It has a population of one hundred and eighty thousand people, and it was once a very important city. You can read all about its ancient beauty and wealth and commerce in the Arabian Nights. Some of the palaces that Harouner Rashid visited are still standing. In the city there are at present sixty-four mosques, six churches and twenty-two synagogues. One-third of the population are Jews, and there are over five thousand Christians. Most of the latter belong to the Roman Catholic faith, or to other twilight churches. The Roman Catholic cathedral, which you see in the picture, is the only church in all Northern Arabia that has a bell. Moslems do not like to hear church-bells, and they were forbidden by some rulers of the Moslem world long ago. The Protestant Christians meet for worship in a dwelling-house. The Bagdad mission has a large dispensary for the sick where thousands of Moslems and Jews and Christians come every year for treatment. Books are sold to the people, and there is a school for boys and girls which is also helping to *turn down* old prejudices and *turn up* the right side of child-life. The Moslem children are beginning to believe that the world is *round* and that Constantinople is not the capital of all Europe.

The British and Foreign Bible Society is also helping to turn this part of the world downside up. The gospel which has been buried under many superstitions and traditions so long, is again showing its power. *Colporteurs* are men who carry the Bible about, offer it to the people and read and explain it to those whose hearts are open. They have a hard task, but if it were not for them the "Little Missionaries" would not get along at all.

On the way from Bagdad to Busrah, we pass Amara, an enterprising village where the people once burned books and threw stones at the missionary, but where now the little Bible-shop of the American Mission shines unhindered,

"Like a little candle, burning in the night."

At Busrah, Rev. James Cantine began mission work in 1891, and ever since that time he and others have been ploughing and sowing seed and waiting for the showers that come before the harvest. It was at Busrah that Kamil Abd el Messiah, the Moslem convert from Syria, died a witness for Christ. Have you read the wonderful story of his life? It is full of pathos and shows how in the heart and life of at least one Moslem the Holy Spirit made topsy-turvy things straight. There are others like Kamil in Arabia, but many of them are still following the Master afar off, because they fear the persecutions of men. At Busrah, there is also a dispensary, and here too the gospel is sold and preached and lived before the people.

Bahrein, you know, is a group of islands, and it is about six years ago that the people first saw a missionary. Nearly three-fourths of the population are pearl-merchants or pearl-fishers. Will you not pray that they may learn to value the Pearl of Great Price?

A visit any morning in the week to the dispensary at Bahrein, would soon convince you that here too the Arab world is slowly but surely turning downside up. Women learn to their delight that they have equal right to sympathy with men, and they need not wait until the men are helped first. The Arabs are very ignorant of medicine and their remedies are either foolish or cruel. To "let out the pain" in rheumatism, they burn the body with a hot iron. All their ideas are upside down, and very few know on which side of their body the liver is located. Now when our mission doctors perform miracles of surgery on the maimed, and miracles of mercy on the suffering, the result is to prepare their hearts for Christ's message. To the fanatic Moslem a Christian is "an ignorant unbeliever." But we may put a parody on Pope's lines and say, in their case:

"A Christian is a monster of such frightful mien
That to be hated needs but to be seen.
But seen too oft familiar with his face
They first endure, then pity, then embrace."

Many of the Moslems who in gratitude are ready to embrace a Christian physician may yet learn to embrace Christian teaching.

Muscat in Arabic, means "the place where something falls." And the surroundings are so rocky and steep that everything has a chance to tumble down except the mercury in the thermometer. That is always up high. In this hot, crowded town, the Arabian Mission opened its third station in the year 1893. Two years before the veteran missionary-bishop, Thomas Valpy French laid down his life here, and the fallen standard was taken up by Peter

J. Zwemer. After five years of toil in Oman, he also entered into rest. George E. Stone, his successor in Oman, was also worthy of the martyr's crown, and his simple grave at Muscat tells how "he arose, forsook all, and followed Christ."

This part of Arabia is sacred because of what these three pioneers suffered to open the door for the gospel. I do not think the King will leave a province where He has buried so much treasure in the hands of the enemy, do you? The work of preaching in Oman is at present full of promise, and the people seem willing to hear. The American Bible Society is sending the Scriptures all over Eastern Arabia.

MUSCAT HARBOUR.

The last mission station in Arabia we mention, is the first that people generally visit. Aden is a coaling station as well as a missionary centre and passengers travelling to the Orient nearly always stop here on the way. There are Christian churches and hospitals and government schools. At Sheikh Ottoman, a short distance from Aden, Ion Keith Falconer, the first modern missionary to this land, began his work. He died here also, but his life was so full of love and sacrifice that his *work* is still going on. The Free Church of Scotland mission has medical work, an industrial school for waifs and a memorial chapel. From a great distance patients come to be cured, and Moslems to buy the Bible.

The great lighthouse on the island of Perim, near Aden, throws its light for ten miles out on the dark sea and saves ships from the breakers. But the light of the gospel in the Bible depot at Aden, shines two hundred miles to the north as far as Sanaa, and three hundred miles east to Makalla on the coast. Yet I dare say it costs more to keep up the lighthouse at Perim (not to speak of building it) than it does to keep open all the Bible lighthouses of all Arabia. Perhaps Keith Falconer thought of this when he said in his farewell address:

"We Christians have a great and imposing war office, but a very small army. While vast continents are shrouded in almost utter darkness and hundreds of millions suffer the horrors of heathenism and Islam, the burden of proof lies upon you to show that the circumstances in which God has placed you, were meant by Him to keep you out of the foreign mission field."

Before you lay aside this book, will you not ask yourself why you should not go out to Arabia, or to some other land yet shrouded in darkness, and shine for Jesus?

An Old Friend in a New Dress.

ARABIC.	LITERAL TRANSLATION.
Seyyidi-'l-Fadi-'l Gani,	Our Lord, the rich Saviour,
Kalbehoo yuhibbooni,	His heart loves me,
Fa lahoo kooloo saghier.	And to Him all little ones belong.
Yaltajee wahoo'l kadeer.	He protects us and is strong.
Kad faaka hubban.	Yes His love exceeds all.
Kad faaka hubban.	Yes His love exceeds all.
Kad faaka hubban.	Yes His love exceeds all.
Yuhibbuna Yasooa.	Jesus loves you.

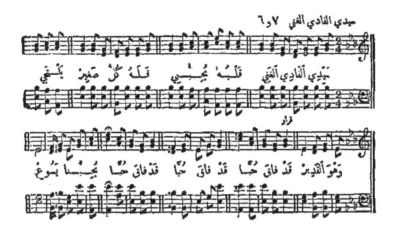

سيدي الفادي الغني   قلبه يجبـي   نلـه كل صغير بنـني

فراد

وهو القدير   قد فاق حبا   قد فاق حبا   قدفاق حبا   يجبنا يسوع